A
Customer
Centered
Company
Culture

Dedications

First and always, I dedicate this book to a loving and caring God of my understanding.

To my little pumpkin Addie, you inspire me to be better every day.

To Jerry and Sheryl Isenhour, you both teach me to be a better coach and trainer but also a better person every day.

Foreword:

Sales is so often a misunderstood word. And even more misunderstood is the word salesman. Often when we envision a salesperson an image comes to mind of a guy in a plaid sport coat, likely smoking a cigar and he is attempting to browbeat us into the submission of acceptance of the product or service he is offering. And often this person simply cannot take no for an answer.

But true sales is not selling the things that people do not want, rather true sales is offering them the products and or services that they are looking for to deliver one of two goals. One is the eradication of a pain that they are undergoing in their lives, often research will show that in the range of 70% of people will make a purchase for this purpose, to eradicate a pain. The other 30% will be looking for a gain or desire, they have their hearts set on something.

And this is where true sales skills come in. It comes from building trust with the customer. Next is the relationship build with the customer. And these things require the person doing the selling to have the skill to listen. Even further they need to understand how the behavior patterns of the buyer often determine the success.

Donovan Blanks is a person who has perfected this and shares his thoughts and processes with you in this book. His principals are sound and will deliver results. To gain the results, one must believe in and implement the processes he shares.

Invest your time into reading this book, I feel that if you do this and give the processes he suggest a try they will deliver sales success to you, the success you envision is as close as implementation of the right processes.

Jerry Isenhour

Inspiration:

When I started writing this book, it originated as building a new concept of how to do business and make sales in the post-pandemic world. Then I was inspired. I had the pleasure of being in small teleconferences with four great speakers.

The first speaker was **Tom Ziglar**. I had grown up listening to his father, Zig Ziglar. I had even met Zig when I was a teenager. Tom's talk took me back to a simpler time. Tom spoke of helping others, and that phrase triggered my idea to define the word *Service.* I instantly had a chapter in this book.

A week later, I was listening to **Randy Pennington** discuss culture and being *Customer Obsessed*. I had never made the connection that what I have been teaching over the last year was culture. I started connecting the dots, and the title of my book was born.

The third week of teleconferencing brought me face to face with **Larry Winget**. Larry never pulls punches and is blunt and to the point. You hear his point of view in a confident and to the point way. Larry will tell you he is not a motivational speaker. Well, I took two things from Mr. Winget. I identified my point of view and my confidence to present it. I also heard the words ***Be Kind and Understanding.*** These are words I use quite often, but they had a deeper meaning suddenly.

The fourth speaker I was lucky enough to listen to, was **Scott McKain**. Scott talked to us about communication and communicating our story. If you can tell your story in a way that other people can connect with, you can make a significant impact on them. Telling my story isn't just in the details. My story must be relatable.

There was a constant thread amongst these four great speakers. I was able to focus on relationship building. I heard from each of them that it's still about the people, and it's always about communication. What I heard was that I was on the right track the whole time and didn't need a new concept. We may need new tools and new processes, but overall, we need the foundation of serving our customers in the best possible ways.

While this book is full of ideas, concepts, and procedures that have worked for me, I would much rather spark your imagination and innovative concepts to start flowing. The steps I have used may not make sense to you at this moment and may never. I am well versed in sales, sales tools, sales closing tactics, types of sales, and sales approaches. While each has a potential place and while each has its pros and cons, I have found value selling and consultation sales to be the most productive in Blue-Collar Industries.

Why? The simplest answer is that few, if anyone, in the Blue-Collar trades want to be considered a salesman. The word often suggests the image of a sleazy used car salesman in a lousy plaid jacket. However, I would suggest that everyone from the janitor to the CEO is in sales. Imagine a process where the entire team understands their value to customers but never feel like they are in sales. The statement that will help create that reality is: "We have a Customer-Centered Company Culture and Sales is a Team Effort."

Next Step? Stop Selling and Start Producing! How? Prepare for the most complicated customer. I can play that role and will do so in this book. Treat every customer with the respect that the most complicated customer would expect.

1. Be Kind and Helpful

The first thing that came to mind as I began planning this book was defining the word service.

serv·ice

noun
1. 1. the action of helping or doing work for someone.
   "millions are involved in voluntary service"

verb
1. 1. perform routine maintenance or repair work on (a vehicle or machine).
   "have your car serviced regularly"

I love definitions, and I love how the meaning of the word service provides exactly how impactful we can be as technicians. The action of helping is such a beautiful way to define what we do. As technicians, we can help others. I hope that adds weight to what you do for a living. I hope that makes you feel important as you read that definition. I hope that makes you feel proud of your chosen profession. We help others, and that's a powerful statement. If you carry that concept with you daily, you are going to have positive energy and a new confidence that will be well received and well respected by those you encounter.

What are the ways we can help our customers, our communities, our families, and our industries? The first thing that comes to mind is education. We can educate our customers about the systems they have. We can provide customers with the best practices for operating their appliance or system in the safest manner possible. We can explain the function of the many different components of a system and how important it is that they all function correctly in conjunction with one another. We can present homeowners with warning signs to look for with specific components and a plan of action should they notice these warning signs. After all, we want the customer to have the safest system possible. We all know we cannot provide a safe system, but continued service of an optimally performing system will provide a safer product.

How can we help our communities? The most reputable companies I come across in the broad umbrella of the service industry are getting the word out to their community. Often in the form of Public Service Announcements. I enjoy it when I see a company bringing awareness to the importance of the sub-industry they are within. Many of these companies stress learning about the importance and safety associated with having routine maintenance performed on the appliances and systems within their home. Staying focused on the best interest of the public is always a great way to educate your community.

I see several companies go a step further and bring awareness to additional issues within the community. I take notice when I see campaigns associated with local and national charities. I often make the connection that when a company promotes a charity, they have somehow been affected by the cause in some way. Being charitable speaks to me on a deeper level, as does the bringing of awareness to the communities we are working and living among. I will often do business with not just the leaders in their respective industries, but the leaders of the community I live in.

We can also educate within our industries, and most sub-industries have excellent training and certification programs. Leaders in an industry will often help bring education even to their crosstown competitors. Education within your industry often provides a level playing ground. Leaders lead, no matter who is following them. We don't give our secrets away, but if we can all work together in any way, it makes us all the better as a whole, and those are the types of people I want to do business with.

How do we educate our families? I know I often took home safety practices. Even with the simplest of tasks at home, I would go to extra lengths to perform the said task in the safest way possible. My work spilled over into my home life in this positive way. I was also now able to answer questions for my extended family members about problems they were experiencing with their appliances and systems. I was able to, in some instances, get them set up with companies in their areas that provide similar or like services as the ones I had become accustomed to providing. It continues to amaze me to this day how positively our work experiences can bring awareness to friends and family. There's a level of passion for your chosen field when you learn the ins and outs of it.

Continually maintaining the mindset of "what can I do for my customer" makes for an excellent opportunity to build a relationship. The service we provide is equally as important. Are we providing a first-time service of an appliance or system or are we providing annual or routine service? I highly recommend that no matter why we are there, that every customer gets the same level of care. The level of care should not be dependent on which neighborhood the house is in, what type of car is in the driveway, and whether we are visiting the house for the first time or the fifth time.

2. Website Presence

We have identified how we can be of service while providing service. Keep in mind the items previously discussed. I am looking for these principles to be prevalent with the company I choose. I have seen the advertisements, I have heard of the company, well now I am going to investigate them by going to their website, social media pages, and reading their google reviews. Luckily for me, as a consumer, all of these things are readily available to me right from my phone. It doesn't take much in today's world to investigate a company and their presence in the community.

I am speaking not only on behalf of the overwhelmingly concerned customer. I am speaking on behalf of most customers, in general, today as it pertains to this issue. If you don't have a website presence, then it's going to be difficult for me to want to do business with you. I want to know all the services a company provides, and if I cannot learn about what your company does from my phone, I'm not going to put forth much more effort. If I can't find google reviews on your company, I am just going to assume that you're hiding the quality of your work. I'm not looking for a 5.0 rating. I am looking for the highest rating from the companies that have the most reviews. I will choose the company with a rating of 4.8 that has 200+ reviews over a company with a 4.9 rating and 15 reviews. I, as a consumer, understand that even the best of companies and people cannot please 100% of the population.

Next, I am going to check your Facebook page. Are you active in keeping your community up to date about what's affecting us locally? Are you informing us about the work you are performing? Are you doing PSAs about your favorite charities, how you are performing services, and what's new in the industry that you work within? Are you telling me the best way to get in contact with you and discuss your services? What kind of specials are you running on your page? I love a deal, and if you have deals, you should be offering them to me here. I am also looking for pictures of your team. Is there anyone on your team that I might not feel comfortable with entering my home?

During this pandemic, I am looking for videos or summarizations of your protocols during this crisis. However, I am not only looking for your crisis protocol; I am searching for previous protocol on your website and social media. I want to know how different your service is today compared to two months ago. Were you careless two months ago and now taking extreme measures to keep yourself in business, or are you making a few simple additions to your protocol because you were already providing exceptional care to your clients? I plan on choosing the business that had excellent protocols in place before the pandemic.

The most impressive thing that I could find on a company's website would be a professionally produced video from an owner or management telling me exactly how they will perform the service I am seeking. I would want to know the details of how they will care for my home and how they will confirm to me what they have done in my home during the appointment. Yes, I would see this as extremely beneficial in preparing for their visit to my home, but I want something to compare my experience. Did I receive the service I was promised in the video? Was I short-changed, or did I get an above and beyond service by my technician? The ownership/management can establish an expectation for me, and that makes me feel extremely comfortable inviting them into my home.

Your website will be the first time you will have contact with many people in today's world. Make a great impression involving your whole team. I want to do business with industry authorities. I want to do business with community authorities. What is distinctive about you? What am I getting from you that I cannot get somewhere else.

3. Office Staff

You hooked me with your great website and social media presence. Now what? Do I call you? Did you grab me in a chat box while on your website or Facebook page? These are all options I am perfectly agreeable to. As I said, you have earned your chance to work for me at least once. I am evaluating the experience every step of the way now. I am grading you. I have started making my decision about doing future business with you. I may not know what that entails at this point, but my process has started.

I am never sure what to expect when I am on the phone with a company's scheduling department. I get so many different experiences when I call a company and speak with their gatekeeper. That is the unfortunate perception of many people that the schedulers are gatekeepers. Why would our customers or the public, in general, view them in this way? They are able to protect the company's reputation. We often conclude that we are getting a phone voice from this person, and they are over-eager to make a sparkling impression. I want an authentic experience every step of the way.

There is a person at a company I work with, and I wish I could name her. She is authentic every step of the way. Her voice and personality are the same on the phone, in the shop, and on camera. She is 100% authentic, and I enjoy this about her. She is energetic and smiling most of the time. You can sense her positive energy over the phone, and it is no act. She is precisely the type of person I would like to have contact with by phone when calling a company for service. Her authenticity is something we should all strive towards. I find myself falling into the trap of using a phone voice periodically.

While I love good energy and I talk about it a lot, that is not enough for me to

want to feel confident in doing business with your company. I need more, and it comes in the basic knowledge and understanding of what the service will entail. You know what? I want more than simply basic knowledge. Nothing upsets me more when common questions cannot be answered over the phone. If it upsets me, I promise it upsets other customers.

I expect you to be able to tell me exactly what I was told online. I will have forgotten the majority of what I learned; however, my memory will be quickly triggered by you being able to repeat, in the same language, what I read or heard on your website. I could also be the type of person who has your website open in front of me during my call to confirm that everyone is on the same page at your company.

I am always impressed with the chimney and venting industry. Many in this industry have an office staff that has passed chimney sweep certification tests. Then add that many have spent a few days out on the truck shadowing the sweeps. What a great way to develop a firm understanding of what is performed out in the field. I know office staff that could walk right onto a truck and sweep chimneys if need be. Think about that for a minute. What a great culture that is.

Know how many points of inspection there are for each type of inspection your company offers. Know the prices of the services your company provides. Know what comes at the price. Are there additional complementary services your company offers? Tell the customer. Is there a checklist report and a narrative report that come with your service? Do you provide pictures? Sell the value of the service and establish an expectation.

4. Time in a Bottle

Put Jim Croce in the queue…

I have heard person after person describe their time as more valuable to them than their money. I have come to believe in this point of view as I have gotten older. I'm not very old, I am still considered a young man by most, but every day you survive, certain things become more relevant to you. My viewpoint has changed on many issues over time, but I do not expect to change this one. If I lose money, I can find a way to make more money. It may be as simple as going to the job I already have, working overtime, or saving a little under the mattress. No matter what it is, I can figure it out and put a plan into action to make more money.

When it comes to time, I have not figured out a way to get that back yet, and there is some information I would like to go back and share with a younger version of myself. Time to me is the most valuable commodity in the world. I want more time with my daughter, I want more time with friends and family members that have passed away, but to my knowledge, there is no such thing as a time machine. I imagine if there were a time machine, someone would have fast-forwarded through 2020. Time Travel is above my paygrade, so I am just trying to enjoy what I have experienced thus far.

The point is that I expect people, especially those in business, to respect and value my time. I want our appointment confirmed by whomever in your office does that for you. I want updates if you are running behind or if you need to reschedule. The worst thing you can do with me is calling me at the scheduled time or after the scheduled time to let me know you are running late. I am the type of person that would tell you, thank you, but no thank you. If I cannot trust you to show up on time for a scheduled appointment, can I depend on you to show up at all if I need work done on the system or appliance you are supposed to service? I truthfully believe showing up is 90% of life, and you better be on time to work for me.

I expect a phone call when you are en route to my home. It gives me time to make simple preparations for you. I have a life and very well could be taking care of something important before your arrival. I've been known step out to the store or run errands in an attempt to utilize the time I have probably taken off work for our appointment. I have been known to doze off and take a nap while waiting for people to arrive. Do you want to get off on the wrong foot with me? Show up to my front door unannounced.

5. First Impressions

Assuming you have followed my recommendation and called ahead to let me know you are in route to my home; I will be awaiting your arrival. I will be somewhere in my house that I will be able to see you as you pull into my driveway. I will be monitoring you before we ever make face-to-face contact. Why? Because I am nervous about having people in my home and I am evaluating you and what type of person you are in the chance that I need future service from you and your company.

Why am I paying such close attention? Several reasons. Are you arriving only to sit in my driveway to finish a call to whomever? Are you completing a text message or a cigarette? Are you looking for items in your truck because you are unorganized? Is the dash of your vehicle cluttered? I am looking to get a glimpse of the cargo area of your truck as well. How well maintained is the back of your vehicle? How organized are you? These things, if I can catch a view, tell me how efficient you are as a technician and as an employee. It tells me whether I can trust you to perform the work that needs to be done and that you care. It provides me with a sense of trust if I happen to leave you alone in my home for any period.

Why do these things matter to me? I do not believe an unorganized or ill-prepared technician is going to be a clean and careful technician. If you are unwilling to adequately take care of the vehicle that provides a living to you, it's hard for me to believe you will take great care of my property and home. Am I overprotective of my house, property, and family? You bet your sweet bippy I am. My home is the most significant investment I have made, and it protects my family.

I am judging you from the moment you step on my property. I am not judging your character, I am not judging what type of son/daughter, father/mother, or brother/sister you are, but you better believe I am deciding how professional you appear to me from a distance. I am willing to cancel our appointment based on what I see as you arrive and get out of your vehicle. I am nervous and scared to death about allowing people into my home, and I am now taking extreme measures to protect the wellbeing of my family, my home, and my health. You could be one of the most exceptional people on the planet, but appearances are everything.

6. Gaining Access

Now you are approaching my home, and I can promise, I am watching you. I am paying attention to what you are carrying to my door. This insight is providing me an opportunity to decide if I am going to allow you into my home. It allows me to compare what I see with my own two eyes with how I was told you'd arrive from your website, Facebook page, or the person I scheduled our appointment. Is everything matching up? Do I see you bringing floor protection to my door? Do I see you carrying rubber gloves, a mask, shoe booties, and disinfectant? I am expecting to see you walking to my door with many if not all, of these items.

How I judge your arrival at my front door is my last chance to decide about allowing you into my home. I can tell you that I don't want to see a dirty technician. I have no idea where you have been prior to

arriving at my home, and if you are dirty. I
am seriously considering stopping you at
my front door if I see indicators that put my
home or health at risk. I also don't want to
see an old dirty hat atop your head. I am
overly cautious at this point, and
cleanliness is of utmost importance to me.

I am concerned about letting you in my
home if you have facial hair. I am referring
to any facial hair. As I sat alone in isolation,
preparing for this book, I was able to do
some research on several disease-related
topics. As I scoured the internet, I found
article after article about how dirty facial
hair is (even trimmed and maintained
facial hair). Guess what I read in every
article and every study. I found that even a
well-trimmed and kept beard of any type
carries more bacteria, viruses, parasites,
and disease than a dog or even the
average farm animal. I don't even know if
the story is factual at this point, but I just
saw all over the news that a Tiger tested
positive for the coronavirus.

I don't want to see you bringing in all
your equipment on your first trip to my

front door. At this time, you are supposed to bring minimal items and introduce yourself. I expect all precautions to be taken before bringing in any of your equipment. I don't want any of your equipment touching my floor or other items in my home before you set up for the service with floor protection. I expect drop cloths and runners laid down for protection before the service and before your equipment is brought into my home. I believe that in this new normal, you are probably taking great care to keep your equipment clean, but that doesn't negate my desire to keep it off my floor and clear of any of my possessions. My hang-ups and rules aren't just about me; it's about my family, and to be fair, you as a technician should have a similar viewpoint. I imagine most of you have families to consider as well.

7. You May Enter

You have passed my initial guidelines; I have decided to answer the door when you get there. It is probably going to take a significant mistake on your part to keep me from allowing you entry at this point. That mistake could come as I come to the door. To some extent, I expect social distancing to continue in some form, and it starts at the door. I am hoping that you will keep your distance from the door, allowing me to open it and begin conversing with you from a respectable distance. Please do not crowd my door. I always find stepping back and allowing space a good practice.

I am a hand shaker; I grew up on the concept of providing all people a good handshake. The handshake is the most commonly used physical greeting for establishing a relationship with people you have never met and widely accepted as a friendly gesture to those you already know. It's also widely recognized as a parting display of affection, courtesy, and a sign of agreeing with each other. I have used it all my life as a gesture of good faith, a symbol of closing a deal, and a way of sizing people up.

Archaeological ruins and ancient texts show that handshaking was practiced in **ancient Greece** as far back as the 5th century BC; a depiction of two soldiers shaking hands can be found on part of a 5th-century BC stone slab on display in the **Pergamon Museum**. The handshake is believed by some to have originated as a gesture of peace by demonstrating that the hand holds no weapon, back in the **caveman** days. However, the Romans who liked to hide daggers in the arms of their robes used to grab each other's sleeves when they met, to figure out the other's intentions.

The use of this historical gesture came to a screeching halt in March of 2020. Today it is considered a top transfer of germs, bacteria, and disease. It seemed as though it happened overnight, and in reality, it did happen overnight for me. As I left North Carolina after a training, I shook hands with the whole team of employees at the company I was working with. The next day as I arrived in New Orleans very few people were shaking hands. Even people I had known for years were passing on handshakes because of the coronavirus. The most common friendly gesture I have ever known was erased from society in the blink of an eye. This saddens me in many ways, but I can tell you that I am not going to shake your hand when you arrive at my home. Eliminating the handshake isn't about what I have always known; it's about protecting my family, home, and my health.

We still have many ways to show respect through physical gestures without touching each other. You may find them awkward and gestures that you have rarely seen in person. A slight bow and head nod when greeting someone is a great way to say hello physically and show respect to the person you are introducing yourself. If you are feeling fun, use the wave Forrest Gump used when he saw

Lieutenant Dan on the dock. Waves, head nods, bows, and the tip of your hat are old ways of saying hello and showing respect, and we have to consider these as new ways to build the relationship. We will no longer be able to start with our trusty handshake.

8. Lend Me An Ear

Joe Cocker might sing you a song….

You have made it into my home, you have overcome my strictest of guidelines, and I am becoming impressed. Don't mess it up. You better have shoe booties and surgical gloves you are putting on as you enter. The drop cloths that I am expecting you to have to protect my floor and home should be neatly folded and have the appearance of being clean. If you come to my door with drop cloths wadded up or they appear to be dirty, I am going to question you about them. I am going to flat out ask if those are fresh or how many times you have used them today. I may ask you to get new ones.

You can ask anyone that I have ever worked with, worked for, or trained that day one, minute one, was folding drops and runners. I am OCD about preparation, and it greatly benefitted me in the field. My drop cloths were always, and I mean always neatly folded. When I approached a front door, I carried these neatly folded drop cloths and runners as a symbol of excellence. I tucked them neatly under my arm like I was presenting the American Flag. This type of approach breeds confidence and excellence in a person. It means you take pride in what you do, and that is contagious.

Now we are probably close enough as you pass by me into my home that I can get a perfect look at your clothes. I will now be able to identify if you smell clean. Smell Good Sell Good. That quote of mine started as a joke, but I was quickly able to identify that it wasn't just humorous, it was a serious point of contention for some customers. I would say it could cause a real problem with a customer if I had an odor that I was carrying around with me. Think about how you step back from odors and often make faces when you smell something disagreeable. It also makes me question how sanitary you are, and I believe that's the first instinct of most people. I'm not going to ask you to leave or stop you from coming into my home at this point, but I am going to hold onto these thoughts, and I may already be reconsidering using you or your company again in the future.

I am going to assume you know why you are in my home, and after our greetings, I expect you to ask me where the appliance or system is that you are here to service. Mind you, I may not know what I have, but I expect you to have at least a vague idea as to why you are in my home. As I lead you to the system or appliance, I expect some level of chit chat as an attempt on your behalf to build a relationship with me. As we arrive at the system or appliance, I expect you to engage with me about what I know of the system. I often used the following questions as a starting point with my customers.

1. How old is the home?
2. How long have you lived in the home?
3. Is the system or appliance original to the home?

4. How often do you use the system or appliance?
5. What issues, if any, are you having with the system or appliance?

*Question Four is not a question I am going to ask if I am servicing much outside of a fireplace or hearth appliance.

*Additional questions may be prevalent depending on what you are there to service.

These questions should give you some good insight into the customer and what their needs and desires are. It allows me to learn about you being an expert technician, and it will enable you to build your authority with me. As you build your authority with me, you are also building my trust in you. Don't try to blow me away with technical terms because I can promise you; I probably won't understand. Simply talk to me and show me you know what you are doing.

You are presented with a small window of time to make a great first impression. I am convinced that you cannot earn a contract during this time. However, I am sure you can lose the opportunity to earn a contract during this time.

A person's favorite topics of discussion are as follows. Themselves. People love to talk about themselves. If you allow me to talk about you or me, I will choose me. People love talking about their homes. Remember, their home is generally their most significant investment, and it's where many of their memories took place. People love talking about their children. I love talking about my daughter and will do so for extended periods if given the opportunity. People have always been and will always be more impressed by someone willing to listen to them talk about topics of importance to them than listening to someone talk about the same topics.

Be a sounding board to your customer. Be willing to simply listen. You might just learn something important about them as a person. We are having a tough year as people. Some people may just want to be heard and allowed to dump some pent-up opinions and feelings. You have a friend if you are willing to listen.

9. Set Your Stage

It is time to set up and get to work. I am going to be paying close attention to how you set up for the service. I am looking for how you respect my property and your work. I find that most technicians who take pride in how they set up for the service also take pride in their work. If I see you take great pride in protecting my home, you are quickly gaining my trust and respect. It tells me a lot about your company as a whole. It tells me that if I need work done as a result of what you find during the service that I can trust; you will set up the same to perform repairs. I also trust at this point that anyone else from your company follows the same standards and will take great care of me and my home.

Remember, I am somewhat of a hard customer, but I expect an explanation of the service in some detail and in what steps you will be performing the service. I am comparing your explanation to the one I received from your website or your office people. Is the description similar? I hope so, I don't expect any two people to use the same language and verbiage, but there ought to be as many parallels as possible. I have high standards, and I am basing my expectations on what I have had explained to me thus far. If you leave anything out, I will most likely ask questions, and one of the best things you can do for me is asking if I have any questions about what you are going to be doing moving forward.

I am most likely going to leave you alone to perform your work now unless I have decided you are not meeting my expectations, or I don't trust you. I may hangout purely out of curiosity, and some people will, but if you have a helicopter customer, there is a good chance you have not eased their concerns about allowing you into their home. This type of customer may be aware of a problem but was unable to identify it themselves. This customer, including myself, will often stay close and watch you perform your job. If I am aware there is a problem; I want to know what the source of the said problem is as soon as possible and what the solution is. I will borderline pester you if this is the scenario.

There are only two ways to deal with this type of customer. The first seems to be the least confrontational and the most appealing to the customer. That is simply explaining as you go what you are inspecting and what you are finding. There are a few problems with this approach. My number one concern in this scenario is that it can be challenging to establish standard commination cues with the customer when you are doing two things at once. It may be difficult for you to give the proper body language and is usually challenging to make good eye contact with your customer. I will let this slide if I am your customer. I am not as concerned about your communication style as I am with you getting to the bottom of my problem.

There is a significant issue with giving what I call the presentation of findings during the service. If you give me too much information at a slow, steady pace, it can build anxiety with me. We are only talking about problems in this process, and there is a long delay in getting to solutions. It's like slowly pulling off a band-aide, and it hurts.

Now take into consideration that you give me a cause for a defect as you find it. There are often multiple potential causes for a defect, and you don't have the whole puzzle put together at this point. Imagine having to backtrack and change your diagnosis after finding more information further into the inspection. Imagine how that looks to your customer. I can tell you that it lessens your authority as an expert in my mind. Why would you give me an explanation only to change it minutes later?

You can simply tell your customer that I want you involved, and I want you to see as much of what I see as possible, but it's hard to give complete answers as we go. It doesn't paint the whole picture. When I complete the assessment, I will be putting a report together, and, in that report, we will be able to put the entire puzzle together. It feels confrontational, but it is the farthest thing from being so. I would argue an overwhelming number of your clients understand it. Let them know that just identifying an issue is only the beginning, we want to get to causation, and we need to complete the entire assessment to do so.

Remember, I am probably your most challenging customer. Still, I will tell you that I much appreciate your explanation that you are not just here to identify problems or defects in the system or appliance. I will appreciate that you are here to do a thorough examination and find the root cause of any issues you find. This builds an excellent level of authority and professionalism with me. I am becoming more and more comfortable that you are an expert technician. You are continually building my trust and respect by being such a professional.

10. Protect Yourself

Depending on what is going on in my home or what I must accomplish with my day, I may or may not leave you to complete the service at this point. If you have followed the previous steps and built a healthy level of respect and trust with me and I am working from home or have chores to do, I will probably go back to performing those duties and leave you be to perform your job. I trust that you will provide me excellent documentation and a well-explained presentation of findings after you complete the assessment. If I am stuck home with the family, I love them beyond all belief, but there is a good chance I will use your presence as an escape. In that scenario, I will back off and watch from a distance as you perform your work. In either situation, you need to feel comfortable in performing the same service, whether being watched or not.

Now is your chance to shine whether I am watching or whether I have left you alone. You have the opportunity to provide the 5-Star service that is expected by every client. I don't necessarily know everything you should or shouldn't be doing, but I have a good idea of what working hard looks like. I can tell if you are focused on the task at hand or whether your mind is somewhere else. If I am watching you, I am looking for you to have a system of how you perform your job, a system that at least appears to flow well from task to task.

Don't be surprised if I have a few questions as you go. Some of my questions might be meaningless questions, and some may carry more weight than I realize. Be prepared to answer each of my questions as though they are essential. How you answer even the simplest of questions tell me a little about you as a person, it tells me how professional you are as a technician, and it shines some light on your level of expertise. I am mostly concerned with how you are treating me as a person at this point, but it allows you to stand out.

Remember, every situation is an opportunity to learn and grow not only as a technician or an expert but as a person. Take advantage of every opportunity.

I imagine you are now moving your equipment in or already have it in at this stage. I imagine you are putting on personal protective equipment as well. I imagine no matter the level of danger with the associated service, there are some levels of protection a technician takes. I may again have questions; to some extent, many of your customers, including myself, are curious children who have no idea what exactly you are doing and or wearing in my home. I will tell you that if you are taking significant measures to protect yourself, my level of respect for you is growing. It tells me about you as a technician and a person, but it tells me a lot about the culture of your company. I tend to believe those that protect themselves well are also protecting my family and my home from danger.

I have always viewed respect as a triangle. The triangle is the strongest geometrical shape unless you remove one of its legs. If you remove one of the legs of a triangle, like having a two legged bar stool; there are unknowns, the strength is gone, and it is no longer stable. Let's add respect to the formation of a triangle. If you respect yourself, I believe that you will respect others and their property. If you respect yourself and others, I think they will respect you in return. You, as a technician and as a person, are responsible for two legs of the respect triangle. If you provide those two legs of the triangle, it is believed by myself and others that there is no choice for the majority but to provide the third leg of the triangle. In my opinion, building this triangle is how you form an unbreakable bond with people in every aspect of life.

11. Make It Memorable

I am your most challenging customer, and to be clear, even if I am still in the room watching you perform your duties, I have probably started putting my focus elsewhere. I have probably begun utilizing my phone, answering work emails, looking at things I must do over the next days or weeks, and I may even be playing games or talking to people. Either way, I am still taking the periodic gaze in your direction. I'm keeping an eye on you even though I have moved onto other things. Besides, if I wanted to watch you in a way that would provide me the most information, I would just go to my office and turn on a camera and see how you are performing under the assumption I am not watching. Keep that in mind, folks. Many people have cameras all over their homes. You may just be on a hidden camera.

I am a proponent of checklists. Why? For three primary reasons. I teach technicians, in many instances, how to conduct inspections. You may perform 27 points of inspection to 70 points of inspection depending on the system and or the type of appliance. I, as an educator, can forget points of inspection from time to time if I do not have a checklist to follow. Many appliances are different, and many systems are different; that often leads to different points of inspection. I am by no measure the leading expert in any industry, but the people that have taught me to be an expert have always recommended a checklist of some sort to prevent missing points of inspection.

In many instances, with the performance of inspection on a system or appliance comes substantial liability. Having a point of inspection checklist is of paramount importance for your documentation records. It can significantly reduce your liability when you can prove what you inspected via this type of document. Something terrible happening, which results in damage or loss in one of our customers' homes, is a nightmare. Add to that nightmare that we missed a point of inspection, and it confirms the need for a checklist.

Back to your customer, I can tell you that I expect a checklist, or a point of inspection list associated with your service. Why? It tells me what you have done and what you have inspected. I probably have no idea what much of your checklist items are, but I hope to by the end of the service. Generally speaking, when I have a company provide service to me, I want to learn as much as possible about my appliance or system that you are servicing. I expect you as an industry expert to educate me on my appliance or system. I always assumed that the clients I dealt with wanted to learn about their systems and appliance, or they would not have had me out to perform service. The assumption is dangerous but taking this idea with you into every home will get you better reviews and more contracted work for repairs.

12. Impressive Report

Now we are getting somewhere, you have completed a 5-Star service, filled out a point of inspection checklist, you've taken great care of my home, you have cleaned up nicely, and I can't tell you had even been in my home. What's next? It's time to take all of our documentation and write a summary report for our customers. Why doesn't the checklist and a verbal explanation suffice? There are several great reasons, and of course, I will explain.

While a checklist can provide great documentation of what we inspected, it doesn't usually give enough information to our customers to make an educated decision about repairs or to become well informed about their system or appliance. We need to go deeper. I believe we are all educators as technicians in any service industry, and a checkmark showing a component as suitable or defective just doesn't cut it.

I have developed a way to explain both in writing and verbally defects in a system or appliance that truly educates your customers. I believe that it is of utmost importance to have your written summary report and your verbal presentation to be as close to identical as possible. I believe that you need to both write and verbalize in great detail the defects of a system or appliance. Why? A client may not recall everything you say as it can be overwhelming if not explained properly, but your client will most likely reread your written report as they seek a greater understanding of their issues. In that instance, your report continues to talk to your client after you have left their home. Make it good!

What is the purpose of your written report and your verbal presentation? It has several purposes. First and foremost, you will have in detail your verbiage of why you are recommending that the system or appliance is not suitable for use as intended. The written report can be a key component in passing the burden to act to your customer.

Last time I checked, we still live in the United States of America, which is still a free country. Keeping that in mind, many people may be of the mindset that they will continue to use their system or appliance regardless of recommendation. Therefore, it is important to document in writing why you are recommending they shouldn't. You will be met with an instant brick wall if you tell me I cannot do something with my property in my home. I am much more likely to listen to recommendations.

If you are not only a service company, but you also provide repairs to defects that you identify, your written report and verbal presentation of findings take on an additional purpose. The presentation is your opportunity to form an agreement with your customer that not only is there a defect but that the defect is one that will need repair before future use. Forming this agreement is a difficult proposition for many, but it doesn't have to be. I have created a simple outline that takes you through this process. There are five steps to this process.

First, you must be able to describe the defective component's original purpose within the system or appliance. Explaining the defect should not be difficult as a trained technician and expert in your industry. The industry certification tests that I am familiar with require you to know the anatomy of the systems you will work on, and many appliance manuals provide this information for you at least to some extent. When you write and verbalize to your customer, you are building on your authority as an expert and professional.

Second, what is the defect? You found it; you better be able to describe it to your customer. In all seriousness, this is the simplest step of the process, simply detail the defect as well as you can. What it looks like and supporting pictures will help you quite a bit. If you didn't explain where in the system the defect was found, now is a great time.

The third is an opinion of what caused the defect and is incredibly helpful to most people. Most people are already wondering how it happened, and before developing this step into my presentation, it was the most common question I answered. There could be multiple reasons, or you might have pinpointed the cause based on the other evidence you found during your inspection. If you are not certain or are unable to form a supported opinion, list all the reasons, and be honest with your customer that you didn't find the supporting evidence for an opinion. We are at the stage with the customer that they are very understanding and appreciative of honest answers.

Fourth, you have to be able to explain in written and verbal form what the potential risks are to continuing to use the system with the identified defects. This information is not an opportunity to scare your customers into contracting repairs with you. Using fear tactics generally paralyze people's decision-making process. However, detailing out every risk as potential is very beneficial. We can never tell anyone that a certain risk is guaranteed to become a reality. If we could see the future, none of us would be working in a position that requires a physical performance if working at all.

Why is this so important? You don't know what is going to get through to any single person unless they have told you exactly what will create urgency for them. Assuming your customer has not told you exactly which potential risk will convince them not to use the system until repaired, we must provide each customer with all of the risks. If you tell me about two potential risks, but there are five, one of three things will happen. I may not view your explanation as serious enough to discontinue use. I may find out via the internet that there were more risks that you didn't share with me, and I will probably lose respect and trust in you as an expert. You may luck out and hit the one I needed to hear, and that could have decided for me. The takeaway is that you don't know which detail is going to get through to your customer, and we need to use them all; it's our job to be detailed.

13. Repairs

The fifth step of the process is the one we will take the most in-depth look into because, in my opinion, it carries the most weight with customers in deciding to move forward with repairs or a new install. The fifth step is making the proper recommendation for repairs.

How do we make the appropriate recommendation for repairs associated with the system we have inspected? As a technician and as a consumer, I do not believe in a one size fits all approach to problems. Remember earlier, when we asked our customers questions about the system and their home? Using the customer's answers should be a basis for what we recommend. We should have taken notes during this simple conversation and paid close attention to not only their direct answers but to any additional information they provided us in conjunction with these questions.

You should have found out how often and how your client uses the system. In the chimney and venting industry, this gives me insight into what type of system or repair would most benefit their lifestyle. Often the answer to this question will include a wish from your client for a different kind of appliance or system. You will often hear, "We love using it on Sundays for ambiance, but we hate the mess and hassle of bringing wood into the house." You may hear, "we love the ambiance, but this unit just doesn't produce any real heat in the room; if it did, we'd use it more." I have been in the field with technicians and heard customers tell us almost exactly what they want. Listening is great if you are listening to your customers to build a greater understanding of them, their needs, and their desires.

It is of paramount importance to know all the options for repair and confirm through simple questioning and price ranging, which option will suit your client best. Your recommendation needs to take into account your client's vision and your client's budget into consideration. By telling them about four to five options, they will take some ownership and begin making decisions on what makes sense to them. By giving them a price range, you keep them in the decision-making process and can eliminate some options immediately. Your customers must feel like they are participating in the process.

If you are presenting me with choices, I want to hear three to five options and a price range for each option. I will zero in on an option based not solely on price but also based on my wants. If you have established my wants and needs with me, not only am I quicker to choose an option for detailed pricing, you have shown me how valuable you are, and I am feeling well respected. I trust you very well at this point, and you cannot put a price tag on that. You will have to upset me or give up, to lose my business now. You may not earn my business today unless you live under a rock; there's a lot of uncertainty in the world, especially when it comes to finances, and you better believe I, as well as your average customer, will use the pandemic as an excuse to not do business with you right now. We will discuss that further in the ensuing chapters. At this point, you haven't even presented me an estimate, so let's get to that next.

14. Presentation

I have presented you with my guidelines for building a relationship based on value, respect, and trust with the toughest of customers. I am, in many ways, your most difficult and most challenging customer to impress. Remember, I am a veteran of the service industry and a blunt person in general. You have come a long way in earning my respect and trust. I am ready to discuss options for repairs to my system. You have done the due diligence, you have my preferred choices for functional repairs, and now I am prepared for detailed pricing from an estimate you have created just for me.

The estimate is the first way we ask a customer for their business. It is passive, but without an estimate, how can we ever expect someone to do business with us?

No one I know will sign a contract based on a price range given in a verbal format.

Your estimate needs to be professional. I know this sounds elementary, but there are things I look for on an estimate. I want to see a nice clean letterhead of some type. I like to see certifications or logos from industry organizations on the estimates I received. I want the estimate I receive to explain the work in great detail; I want to feel like I can explain to someone every step of the repair or installation. I want to know what precautions you will be taking in my home to perform the work safely and in the cleanest way possible. I want to know what you'll be doing with any debris. I want to know every detail within reason, and if it is not on my estimate, I will not do business with you. I do not believe every customer needs the highest level of detail in the estimate, but I think they all deserve it.

In addition to merely issuing an estimate, there are two more ways to begin asking a customer for their business passively. The first is having the standard terms on the estimate. Terms first being the amount your company requires for a deposit on the project to be put on the schedule. Second, being how the remaining balance will be paid. Generally speaking, the balance is paid upon completion. The contracted work will be performed to the customers' satisfaction or in concert with the details of the estimate. Third, there should be an estimated timeline for the start of the work and the completion of the work. If all of this information is put into my estimate, you are pre-answering questions that I am planning to ask of you, and you are telling me how to schedule the work. Believe it or not, this carries excellent value and shows incredible professionalism.

Now for an exciting and often improperly used sales tool. You guessed it. Financing. I try to tell anyone I work with or coach that there are three things we never discuss with customers, they are Politics, Religion, and Finances. Offering financing is a great tool that allows many people to buy more confidently. I propose that your company advertise your financing options or put payment options in your estimates. There is a segment of the population that can and will become offended if you as the technician offer financing as an option in the wrong way. The number one objection to our proposals across all industries is the price. If your instant response is "we offer financing" when faced with a price objection, you are missing your opportunity.

Let me explain. Cost is often a secondary objection and not a primary objection to doing business. In other words, it is not the real objection. When I had a customer object to price, what I heard was they didn't trust me or value what I was proposing. They were expressing a perceived risk and had not received the value they needed to proceed. Some people will never see the value of what you are proposing regardless of how well you present it, but those people aren't our customers. I would often use the price objection as a reason to go over the written report and the estimate again. In my experience, it was often a miscommunication of the details of the proposed work, or I had failed to form the agreement with them. What we discussed in a previous chapter.

I do not see this selling. I don't view this as overcoming an objection. This process is continuing to build and strengthen a relationship with your customer. This process is continuing to build on your value as an industry expert. This process is continuing to build on the value of doing business with your company. This process is continuing to build on the value of the work you are proposing, and it being the right solution to their problems. The instant response of offering financing prevents an opportunity to build a long-term relationship by not genuinely listening to what they are trying to tell you.

You can only get to this point if you are willing to understand each customer on a deeper level. It's not just a job or service you are performing but a relationship you are developing or strengthening. Developing this relationship is about how you treat them with respect.

15. Let's Do The Twist

Like we did last Summer……

Now for a real twist. We have been discussing multiple aspects of how to provide extreme value after performing the cleaning and or inspection of a system or appliance. What about where? Where are we providing the presentation of findings and the presentation of the estimate?

You are reading this as the result of changes to the world. It has brought words into our vocabularies like social distancing. Social distancing applies to our presentations as well as many other aspects of our lives. We are no longer going to be able to sit down at the kitchen table with the majority of our customers. We may no longer be able to take a knee next to them as they sit on their couches and stand shoulder to shoulder scrolling through documents and pictures on our electronic devices may no longer be acceptable.

Many of our customers may no longer be willing to have these close-quarter conversations, and for our safety, we may no longer be able to have such intimate communications. Either way, to provide comfort to everyone involved and because safety guidelines so dictate, we will be communicating virtually for at least the time being. This change may last for months, or it may be the way business is conducted for years to come. No matter the long-term aspects, we have to learn to present our findings and recommendations for repairs in an effective way through virtual means.

We all have some learning to do, and it may seem difficult at first. Talking to a screen and not being able to exchange body language cues with others will be the toughest part for me. I imagine it will be for others. The good news is it should relieve the pressure many of us impose upon ourselves to be perfect in our presentations. We can take our time and, in many instances, read what we have written as we share our screen virtually with our customers. Short term, it might be challenging to get used to, but long term it should refine our ability to communicate in a way that people will have a greater understanding of what we have done during the service and what we have found in the process. If you can maintain the attitude that we are all going to become better at our jobs as a result of learning new ways to perform, you are already winning.

16. Statistics

I want to talk statistics with you for a minute. We used to say that there is only 13-15% of the population with what's known as a High D personality. They are not only decision-makers, but they can make a quick decision if you present them with the facts or details, they require. They do not want a long explanation; they want you to get to the point so they can make the decision. These are the customers that sign on the spot with you during your first visit with them. To confirm, we need to be on our toes in following the processes I have laid out in this book. If we skip steps, these High D personalities will make a quick decision not to do business with us. Just because they are capable of deciding on the spot doesn't mean it will be in your favor.

What we have always taught is how to make the decision-making process simpler and more comfortable for the 80-85%. How did we do that previously? We did that in previous times by providing value every step of the way and providing additional value through follow up phone calls, texts, or emails. In previous times we have not been customer-focused or customer-obsessed until after we missed closing the project on the spot. 40-50% of all closed contracts close within 48 hours from the time of service. At this point, we all become obsessed with trying to close the contract in that 48-hour window, or we give up if we didn't close it at the time of service. There has been little in between.

The fact of the matter is that 80-85% of our jobs close after we have left their home. They come from follow-ups. How we follow up is essential. Pressing a customer to make a decision prevents us from closing the contract later. People have a decision-making process; they must each go through. It is different for each of them. Is there a way you can learn what that process is without becoming pushy? In most instances, we will get an honest answer from a customer with whom we have built a relationship.

If an individual has a decision-making process, and we use sales techniques to get that decision outside of their process, we run risks. The risks are that at some point, they will realize they decided outside of their usual comfort zone. Decisions made by people outside of their usual routine could result in a few different scenarios.

The worst case is we find out that they signed on the dotted line just to get you out of their house because you wore them down. How do we find this out? We show up to work one morning, and the customer canceled the contract. In this scenario, we have lost a contract that we could have maintained had we given them the time to fulfill their process.

There is another scenario that can be equally as bad as the job being canceled. The next scenario is the more common of the scenarios. The customer is going to get even with you for pressuring them into deciding to sign before they were ready.

How do they get even? They become a hassle. They nitpick every aspect of the job and work you for redoes and freebies. They call after the work is done and paid for to have things fixed again. They find anything to complain about. I am aware of at least two companies that use high-pressure sales tactics and have a dedicated callback crew. I don't want that headache, and I doubt you do either.

We have always been trying to add value to our follow-ups. I want to continue teaching that, but we have to present immense value before and during the service if we are going to add value after the service. As I talk to business owners and technicians across the country, we are finding that overall sales are down across the country; however, the closing rates are way up. Why?

Two primary reasons for increased closing rates are as follows. First being that the majority of the customers we are servicing at this time are dealing with a known problem. We do not have to form an agreement with these customers that there is a problem. We simply need to identify the root of the problem and present the proper solution. This type of customer is not at the beginning of the decision-making process. They are formulating a decision and are ready to move forward with the project once they have enough value. Simply showing up to the service provides immense value and maybe what makes the decision easy for the customer.

Second, we are treating each customer as a precious individual. We are transmitting a higher level of value due to the fact many of us around the country are seeing decreased calls. We should have been treating every customer as though they were the most valuable person. This shift is what I have been talking about in this book. If we treat every customer as if they are the number one priority of our company, we are going to be better off long term no matter what is happening in the world.

17. Reaching Out

I am convinced that we cannot sell items or services during this crisis and for the next six to twelve months coming out of the crisis. I am not saying we won't contract work and produce high numbers. I believe many of us will see increased revenues coming out of this mess. I am saying we cannot sell to people. They will buy, and we will do at least as well as we were doing previously.

People are going to be extremely timid. Many are going through financial insecurities and fears of what is to come. If you call me 48 hours after you issued me a quote and asked me if I had looked over the proposal, made a decision, or had questions, you will have turned me off. If you call me to ask how I am doing, how my family and I are getting along during this tough time, and only asking if I received the estimate, I am going to be much more receptive. I will probably chew your ear off and ask you how you are doing. The majority of our customers want high-quality personal service. Many of them have been holed up during this lockdown and wish to have personal contact with people, whether that be by phone, text, or email. You will receive more honest and open communication from your customers when you continually work on building a relationship with them.

I do not believe this approach should be limited to a crisis. I believe that we can learn a lot by merely reaching out to people. We can learn a lot about people and ourselves. Do not give up on this approach in a month when things seem to be going back to normal. This level of care will always make you stand out in every aspect of your life.

18. Summary

I want to end with not only a summarization of the contents of the book, but I also want to end on a positive note. This book may be a lot for many of you to swallow, and it may require a lot of change on your behalf. Still, it will be well worth it if you are going to separate yourself from the competition and come out on the other side as a better company, a better technician, or even a better person.

This change is not just for processes and procedures; this is a change in culture. I was unaware that this is what I've been discussing and teaching over the last year. I heard it yesterday when a well-known coach and speaker talked to a few of us in a round table. I thought all of what I had been teaching and training people was a process, a system, or a procedure. He awakened my eyes to it being a culture, and in the case of this book, a culture change. What I have been doing made more sense than after hearing the explanation during that round table.

The week prior, I was blessed to have been in a round table discussion where another famous speaker and coach talked about helping others. After hearing his talk, it confirmed that what I have been writing about is essential. The definition of service which I started this book with is the component for moving forward and being better not only as individuals but as an industry when we get back to working full time. We will be better as a result of this crisis!

I talk with many technicians around the country every week as a sales coach, dream coach, or a goal coach. I am continually building a better relationship with those I work with. I experienced two separate scenarios that made me very proud over the last week. Two separate technicians stated that it is as if I was preparing them for this pandemic. I have worked with and for some of the greatest minds in the chimney and venting industry. They have been training me to prepare for something like this crisis for the last few years. I have never stopped learning from all the people I have worked with and continued to build a playbook based on what I have learned.

I have never been prouder than to hear the comments that I was helping prepare them to deal with something like what we are currently facing. I was overwhelmingly proud to hear a technician I have been working with for more than nine months was sending out emails to customers just to find out how they were doing during the lockdown. That's first and foremost, the type of caring person he is, but it also lines up with the relationship building we have been teaching. I have had so many proud moments lately.

This book is to motivate and inspire change for the better, not to become better, but to become the best! We are all inspired at times, but we never take a moment to write things down so that they can become real. We are all motivated, but we never take the time to write down what motivates us to become better, and we become motivated to stay where we are. This book didn't become real until I started writing it, and the book wasn't finished until it was finished. Each of us has untapped potential and the ability to become the best version of ourselves, don't let it go to waste by not making it real.

19. Once Upon a Time....

I have a suggested exercise. It can solidify your company culture. Take the time to have a company meeting. In this meeting, tell the story of how you got into the business, how the business started, why you decided to get into the business, and what it means to you today. Employees and coworkers will enjoy this time of communication. Don't make this all about you, though. Use this time to have each employee to tell their story of how they ended up working at your company. What led them to your business and your industry.

Sharing your stories is a fantastic team-building exercise and a culture-building exercise. What an enjoyable way to come together over the company and the industry you are in together.

About The Author.....

The toughest part of the entire book. I have been in professional sales since I was fifteen years old. I grew up in a family business doing small scale kitchen remodels. I was the owner's son, but I had to earn my contracts. I became a student of sales and remain a student today. I have never stopped learning about ways to provide a better product or service to customers.

The service industry and the sales associated can be very frustrating and extremely rewarding. Half of the customers we are working for don't know they have a problem and are none to excited to have me explain a problem and an expensive repair. I went back to listening, I went back to a deeper level of value selling. I educated people in a calm rational and non-blaming way that they would understand. I learned to understand the customer on a deeper level, and I provided solutions that fit their wants, needs, and desires. I provided solutions that alleviated their pains and frustrations. I found great success in this approach.

After developing a process that allowed me to find great success in producing high revenues in the service industry, I found myself being offered a lifelong dream to teach sales. I love selling value and I am a firm believer that anyone who has developed a good industry knowledge can sell value day in and day out. Selling value isn't selling at all to me and it produces the highest revenues.

We have developed a recipe for success in selling chimney repairs and hearth products by focusing on value and customer understanding. The beautiful part of the recipe is that it's duplicatable. It has been so effective that technicians we have worked with are achieving goals to the extent that we are having to establish new goals.

I cannot take responsibility for your successes or failures but, my goal is to play a small part in helping you achieve your goals.

info@CVCSuccessGroup.com

www.CVCSuccessGroup.com

Donovan@CVCSuccessGroup.com

VIRTUAL LEARNING
PLATFORM
CVC
VIRTUAL
ACADEMY